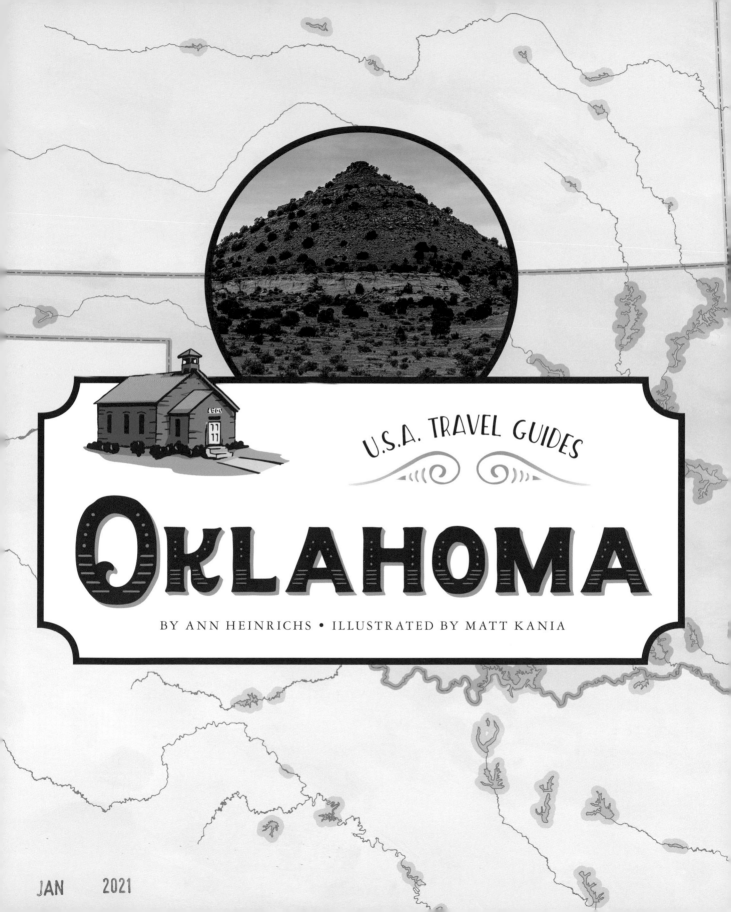

U.S.A. TRAVEL GUIDES

OKLAHOMA

BY ANN HEINRICHS • ILLUSTRATED BY MATT KANIA

JAN   2021

The Child's World®
childsworld.com

Published by The Child's World®
1980 Lookout Drive • Mankato, MN 56003-1705
800-599-READ • www.childsworld.com

Photo Credits
Photographs ©: John A. Davis/Shutterstock Images,
cover, 1; Tom Till/Alamy, 7; Shutterstock Images, 8, 27, 37
(top), 37 (bottom); iStockphoto, 11, 24, 31, 32, 35; Matt
Howry CC2.0, 12, 16; US Army, 15; World Wide Images/
iStockphoto, 19; Dave Stone CC2.0, 20; Josef Mohyla/
iStockphoto, 23; Jeremy Smith/Shutterstock Images, 28

ISBN 9781503819764
LCCN 2016961189

Printing
Printed in the United States of America
PA02334

Ann Heinrichs is the author
of more than 100 books
for children and young
adults. She has also enjoyed
successful careers as a
children's book editor and
an advertising copywriter.
Ann grew up in Fort Smith,
Arkansas, and lives in
Chicago, Illinois.

About the Author
Ann Heinrichs

post card

Matt Kania loves maps and, as a
kid, dreamed of making them. In
school he studied geography and
cartography, and today he makes
maps for a living. Matt's favorite
thing about drawing maps is
learning about the places they
represent. Many of the maps
he has created can be found in
books, magazines, videos, Web
sites, and public places.

About the
Map Illustrator
Matt Kania

post card

*On the cover: The Black Mesa is in
Oklahoma's Panhandle.*

OUR OKLAHOMA TRIP

OKLAHOMA

Get ready for a great adventure. We're heading for Oklahoma! Just follow that dotted line. Or try it your way and skip around. Either way, you're in for a wild ride!

You'll watch tricky horseback riders. You'll see prairie dogs and buffalo. And you'll go speed racing through the sand.

There's lots more to see and do in Oklahoma. So buckle up and settle down. We're on our way!

WELCOME TO OKLAHOMA

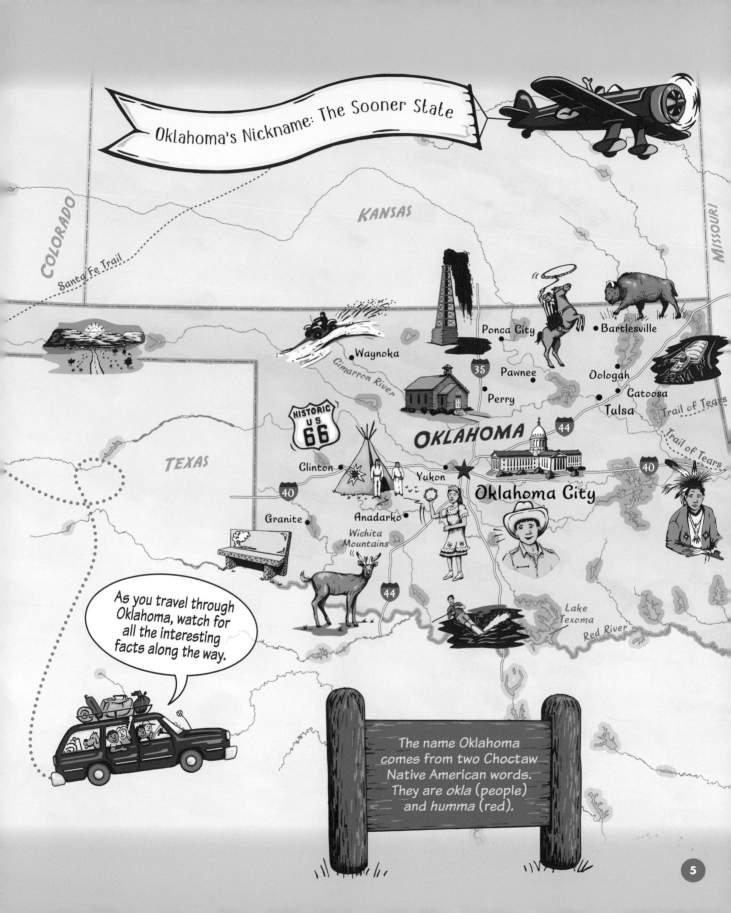

Oklahoma's Nickname: The Sooner State

COLORADO

KANSAS

MISSOURI

Santa Fe Trail

Cimarron River

Waynoka

35

Ponca City

Bartlesville

Pawnee

Oologah

Perry

Catoosa

Tulsa

Trail of Tears

HISTORIC US 66

OKLAHOMA

44

Trail of Tears

TEXAS

40

Clinton

Yukon

Oklahoma City

40

Granite

Anadarko

44

Wichita Mountains

As you travel through Oklahoma, watch for all the interesting facts along the way.

Lake Texoma

Red River

The name Oklahoma comes from two Choctaw Native American words. They are *okla* (people) and *humma* (red).

Can you hike uphill for hours? Then you can hike up Black **Mesa**. It's just outside Kenton, and it's Oklahoma's highest point.

Black Mesa is way out in the Panhandle. The Panhandle is the western part of Oklahoma. It looks like a handle you could grab!

Rolling **plains** cover much of western Oklahoma. But the east is hilly and full of forests. Oklahoma has several mountain ranges, too.

Many lakes are scattered throughout the state. Most were made by building dams on rivers. The Red River runs through southern Oklahoma. The Arkansas River cuts across northeastern Oklahoma. It continues through Arkansas to the Mississippi River.

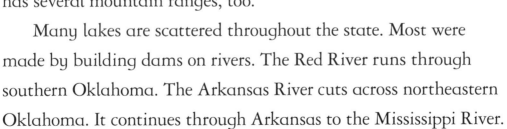

Black Mesa State Park has many different rock formations.

FUN ON LAKE TEXOMA

Do you like water sports? Then head on down to Lake Texoma. Oklahoma and Texas share this huge lake. It's a great place for waterskiing.

If you like doing cool tricks, try wakeboarding. A wakeboard is like a big skateboard. A boat pulls you through the water. Then you do tricky jumps and flips!

Oklahoma's a great place for outdoor fun. People love fishing, camping, and hiking there. The state also has dozens of museums. You can explore history, science, or art. Rodeos and Native American festivals are popular, too. Hundreds of people attend Oklahoma's Native American festivals, such as Anadarko's American Indian Expo. Whatever you like, you'll find it in Oklahoma!

Grab a wakeboard and head to Lake Texoma! The wake is the foamy path of water behind a moving boat.

Wow! Look at that guy doing double back rolls on his wakeboard!

COLORADO

MISSOURI

KANSAS

TEXAS

★ Oklahoma City

• Anadarko

Lake Eufaula

Lake Texoma

Red River

Lake Eufaula is Oklahoma's largest lake in surface area. Lake Texoma is the second largest. It was created by building dams on the Red River.

The Science Museum Oklahoma is in Oklahoma City. You'll explore things such as light, sound, energy, and the stars.

Fifteen buffalo were introduced in the wildlife refuge in 1907. They came from the New York Zoological Park.

KANSAS

COLORADO

MISSOURI

Did you know that some owls can live in a hole in the ground?

STATE FLOWER
OKLAHOMA ROSE

STATE TREE
REDBUD

STATE BIRD
SCISSOR-TAILED FLYCATCHER

Wichita Mountains Wildlife Refuge

TEXAS

Tall grasses used to cover Oklahoma's plains. These grassy plains are called prairies. Farmers plowed up much of the grass. But some still remains for grazing cattle.

The National Park Service has six sites in Oklahoma.

Armadillos and coyotes are often seen in Oklahoma.

WICHITA MOUNTAINS WILDLIFE REFUGE

Want to search for cool animals? Try the Wichita Mountains Wildlife Refuge. It's in southwestern Oklahoma. The animals that live there are protected.

Take buffalo, for example. Millions of buffalo used to roam the plains. But hunters killed nearly all of them. Today, about 650 buffalo live on this refuge. You'll also see deer, elk, and longhorn cattle herds.

You might notice lots of holes in the ground. You've found a prairie dog town! These little critters dig tunnels for their homes. You might see burrowing owls nearby. They build their nests in prairie dog holes!

This family of prairie dogs calls Wichita Mountains Wildlife Refuge home.

WOOLAROC IN BARTLESVILLE

It's a working ranch. It's a wildlife **preserve**. It's a living history museum. Woolaroc in Bartlesville is all these things at once. It's hard to decide what to see first!

The Mountain Man Camp is along one trail. Feel free to hang out with the mountain men in the spring and summer seasons. They'll show you how hunters and trappers lived long ago.

Wind along trails in the wildlife preserve. You'll see llamas, ostriches, and pygmy goats. Those are especially small goats. You'll see buffalo, elk, and cattle, too.

These animals are wild, so don't pet them. But stop by Woolaroc's petting zoo. It has chicks, piglets, rabbits, and goats. You can pet them all day long!

The name Woolaroc *is a combination of three words: woods, lakes, and rocks.*

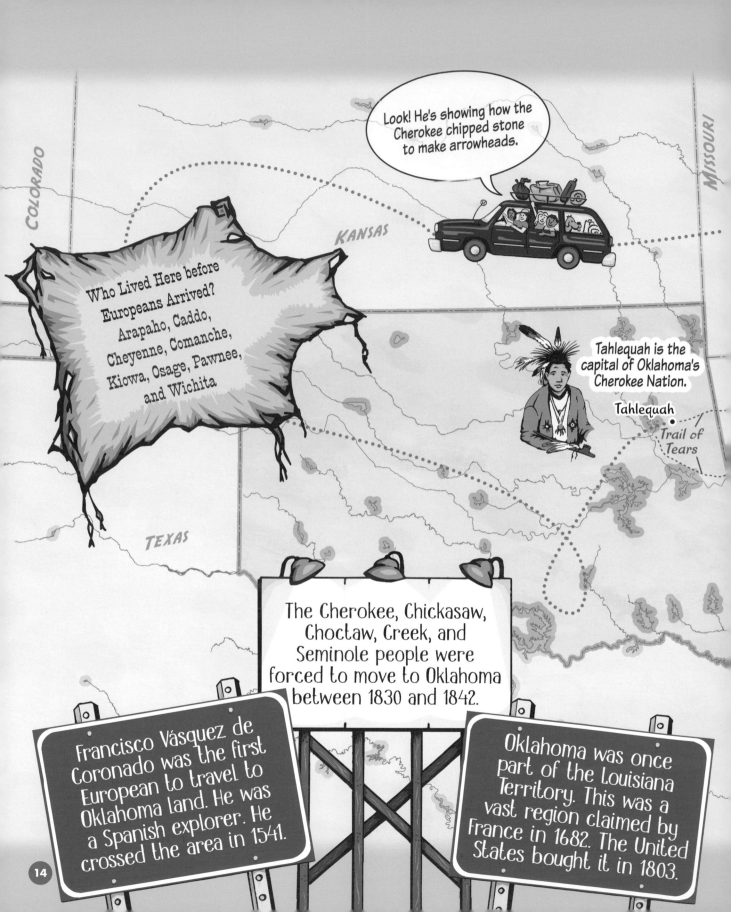

THE CHEROKEE HERITAGE CENTER IN TAHLEQUAH

Your guide is a Cherokee Native American. He shows you how the Cherokee made canoes. He teaches you how they hunted with **blowguns**. Then you can play a Cherokee stickball game!

You're visiting an ancient Cherokee village. It's part of the Cherokee Heritage Center in Tahlequah. There you learn about the Cherokees' daily life.

Native Americans have lived in Oklahoma for hundreds of years. Today, more than 30 Native American tribes are in Oklahoma. The Cherokee Nation in Oklahoma is the largest tribal nation in the United States.

In 1803, Oklahoma land became part of the United States. At that time, much of Oklahoma was declared Indian **Territory**. Native Americans from southeastern states and elsewhere were forced to move there. Thousands died along the way. This journey is known as the Trail of Tears.

Cherokee Native Americans teach visitors about their ancestors' way of life.

ROSE HILL SCHOOL AT PERRY'S CHEROKEE STRIP MUSEUM

The kids are wearing old-time clothes. They file past their stern-looking teacher. Then they sit in pairs at wooden desks. They write on their slates with chalk.

These kids are living in the past. It's just for one day, though. They're attending Rose Hill School. It's part of the Cherokee Strip Museum in Perry.

The Cherokee Strip ran across northern Oklahoma. The U.S. government promised it to the Cherokees. Later, Oklahoma was opened to white settlers. People dashed in to claim land. Many of their kids attended Rose Hill School. Piece by piece, the Native Americans lost their land.

The Rose Hill School still has most of its original furniture.

Shh! Listen to what the teacher has to say.

COLORADO

KANSAS

Santa Fe Trail

MISSOURI

TEXAS

• Perry

Some people sneaked into parts of Oklahoma before they opened for settlement. These people were called Sooners. Why? Because they got there sooner than others! That's why Oklahoma is called the Sooner State.

Settlers, traders, and soldiers crossed Oklahoma on the Santa Fe Trail. It ran from Missouri to Santa Fe, New Mexico.

The Cherokee Strip was opened for white settlement in 1893. This was the largest of Oklahoma's land runs.

Oklahoma's first land run took place in 1889.

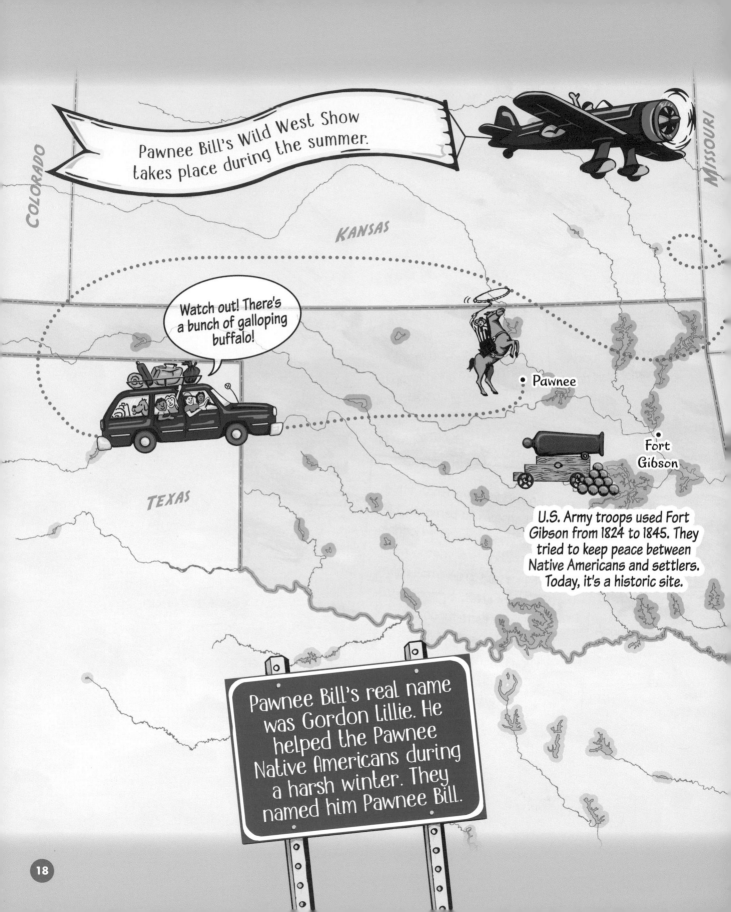

Pawnee Bill's Wild West Show takes place during the summer.

COLORADO

MISSOURI

KANSAS

Watch out! There's a bunch of galloping buffalo!

• Pawnee

Fort Gibson

TEXAS

U.S. Army troops used Fort Gibson from 1824 to 1845. They tried to keep peace between Native Americans and settlers. Today, it's a historic site.

Pawnee Bill's real name was Gordon Lillie. He helped the Pawnee Native Americans during a harsh winter. They named him Pawnee Bill.

Want to meet some real live cowboys? Come to Pawnee Bill's Wild West Show in Pawnee! You'll watch trick riders on galloping horses. And you'll see flashy tricks with ropes and whips.

Pawnee Bill had a ranch near Pawnee. He started a Wild West show in 1888. Western Oklahoma was cowboy territory then. Texas cowboys drove their cattle through Oklahoma. Oklahoma had lots of cattle ranches, too.

The cowboys liked to show off their skills. That's how rodeos began. Rodeos are cowboy contests for riding and roping. Oklahoma still has lots of rodeos today.

Rodeos are popular events in Oklahoma.

OKLAHOMA CITY'S COWBOY MUSEUM

Put on your **chaps** and spurs. Then hop into the saddle. It's time to be cowboys and cowgirls!

You're visiting the National Cowboy and Western Heritage Museum in Oklahoma City. And you're in the Children's Cowboy Corral. That's a really fun part of the museum.

Plenty of real cowboys live in Oklahoma. They work on cattle ranches. Ranching is Oklahoma's main farming activity. Thousands of cattle graze across the state. Most of them end up as beef.

Fields of wheat wave across the plains, too. Wheat and hay are Oklahoma's major crops. Oklahoma also grows lots of pecans.

A statue of cowboys welcomes visitors to the National Cowboy and Western Heritage Museum.

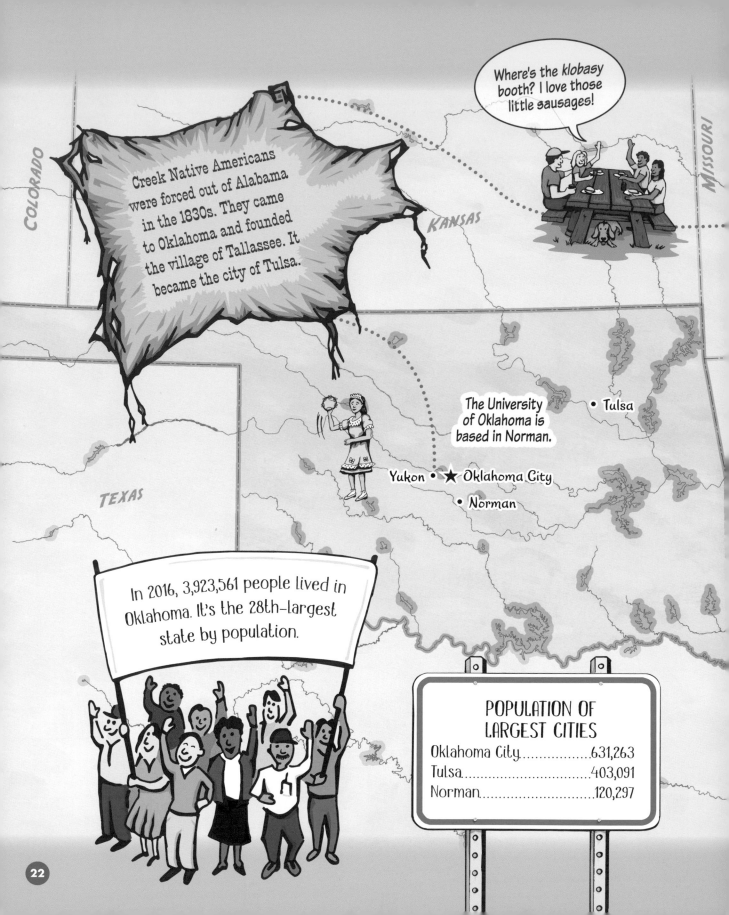

Creek Native Americans were forced out of Alabama in the 1830s. They came to Oklahoma and founded the village of Tallassee. It became the city of Tulsa.

Where's the klobasy booth? I love those little sausages!

COLORADO

MISSOURI

KANSAS

TEXAS

The University of Oklahoma is based in Norman.

• Tulsa

Yukon • • ★ Oklahoma City

• Norman

In 2016, 3,923,561 people lived in Oklahoma. It's the 28th-largest state by population.

POPULATION OF LARGEST CITIES

Oklahoma City.................631,263
Tulsa.................................403,091
Norman............................120,297

THE CZECH FESTIVAL IN YUKON

Kids in colorful costumes are dancing. Lively music's in the air. So are the smells of yummy foods. Try a pastry called *kolache*. Bet you can't eat just one!

You're at the Czech Festival in Yukon. This celebration is held every year in early October. Czechs and Slovaks settled there in the 1800s. They came from Eastern Europe. Their **descendants** still celebrate their **culture** every year.

Many **immigrants** arrived in the late 1800s. They came to work in Oklahoma's coal mines. They came from Russia, Italy, and many other lands. Their descendants add to Oklahoma's rich mix of people.

Children celebrate by dancing during the Czech Festival.

PONCA CITY'S MARLAND OIL MUSEUM

Where does oil come from? Workers drill into the ground to reach it. Sometimes oil comes gushing out. This means that they've struck oil!

Oil became a big **industry** in Oklahoma. Many Oklahoma cities began as oil **boom towns**. One was Ponca City. Ernest Marland found oil there in 1911. Just check out the Marland Oil Museum. You'll learn all about Marland's oil business.

Oklahomans had a hard time in the 1930s. Farmers suffered a drought, or lack of rain. The soil became dry and blew away easily. Thousands of farmers left the state. This period was called the Dust Bowl.

Today, workers still drill for oil in Oklahoma.

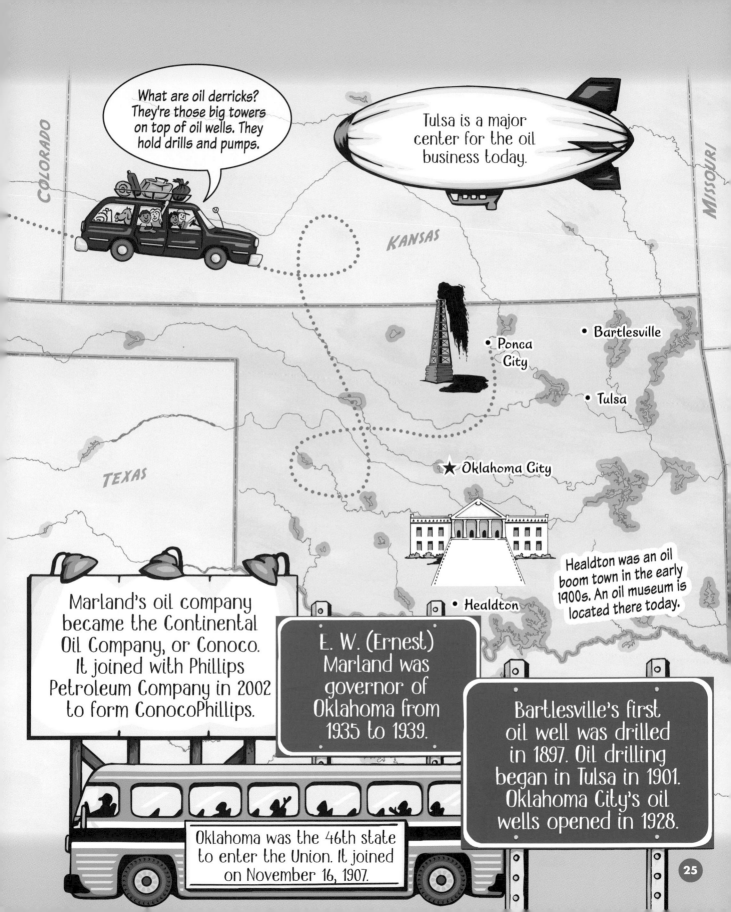

What are oil derricks? They're those big towers on top of oil wells. They hold drills and pumps.

Tulsa is a major center for the oil business today.

COLORADO

MISSOURI

KANSAS

• Ponca City

• Bartlesville

• Tulsa

TEXAS

★ Oklahoma City

Healdton was an oil boom town in the early 1900s. An oil museum is located there today.

• Healdton

Marland's oil company became the Continental Oil Company, or Conoco. It joined with Phillips Petroleum Company in 2002 to form ConocoPhillips.

E. W. (Ernest) Marland was governor of Oklahoma from 1935 to 1939.

Bartlesville's first oil well was drilled in 1897. Oil drilling began in Tulsa in 1901. Oklahoma City's oil wells opened in 1928.

Oklahoma was the 46th state to enter the Union. It joined on November 16, 1907.

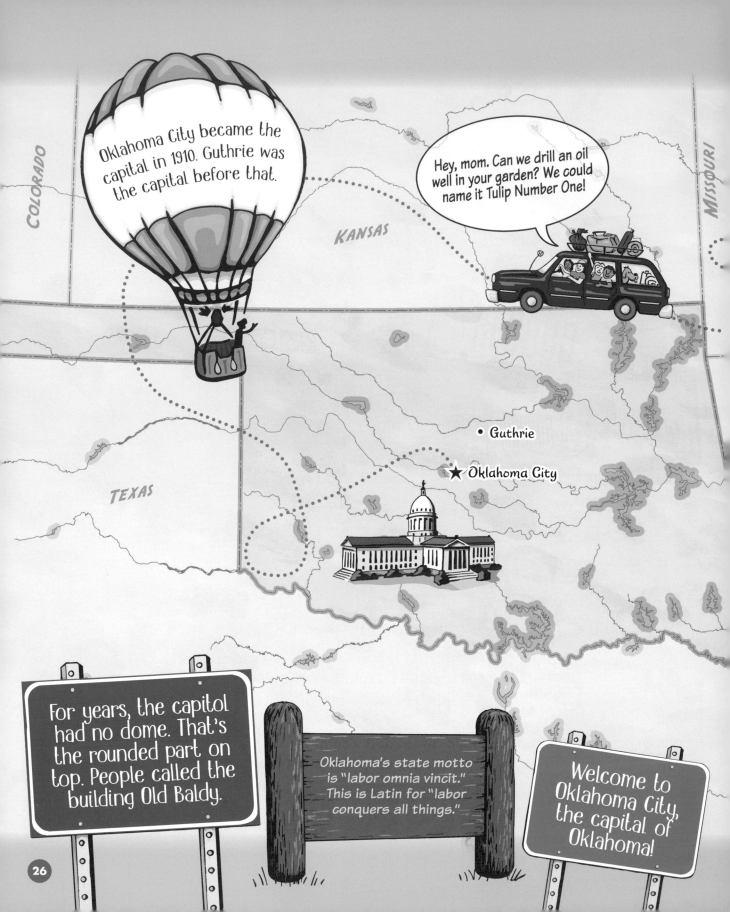

Oklahoma City became the capital in 1910. Guthrie was the capital before that.

Hey, mom. Can we drill an oil well in your garden? We could name it Tulip Number One!

COLORADO

KANSAS

MISSOURI

TEXAS

• Guthrie

★ Oklahoma City

For years, the capitol had no dome. That's the rounded part on top. People called the building Old Baldy.

Oklahoma's state motto is "labor omnia vincit." This is Latin for "labor conquers all things."

Welcome to Oklahoma City, the capital of Oklahoma!

THE STATE CAPITOL IN OKLAHOMA CITY

A strange thing stands next to the state capitol in Oklahoma City. It's an oil well. It even has a name. It's called Petunia Number One. Workers drilled the well in a flowerbed. That flowerbed was full of petunias!

Oil is important to Oklahoma. But the state couldn't operate without a government. Many state government offices are in the capitol.

Oklahoma's government has three branches. The governor heads one branch. This branch makes sure people obey the state's laws. Another branch makes the state laws. The third branch consists of judges. They decide whether someone has broken the law.

Lawmakers are busy in Oklahoma's state capitol.

BARGES AT THE PORT OF CATOOSA

Just take a look at those **barges**. It's hard to believe they're boats. Each one's longer than two basketball courts!

You're down at the Port of Catoosa. It's the end point of a long waterway. That waterway is the McClellan-Kerr Arkansas River Navigation System.

Work began on the system in the 1950s. Workers made the Arkansas River deeper. Locks and dams were built, too. They raise and lower the water level. This allows huge, heavy barges to travel on the river.

The system opened in 1971. This was great for Oklahoma's businesses. They could ship tons of goods by water. That was much cheaper than land or air travel.

Barges are used to transport cargo.

Cool! They tie eight barges together. Then a towboat pushes them along from behind.

The Arkansas River Historical Society Museum is in Catoosa.

Tulsa • • Catoosa

Barges travel the Arkansas River to the Mississippi River. From there, they go south to the Gulf of Mexico. That's part of the Atlantic Ocean.

The jumbo hopper barge is a common type of barge. It measures 35 by 195 feet (11 by 59 m).

The Port of Catoosa is just east of Tulsa.

Tulsa is Oklahoma's major manufacturing center. Its Port of Catoosa is Oklahoma's busiest port.

WILLIS GRANITE PRODUCTS IN GRANITE

You feel like you're in a museum of stone. Some things you see are tall, like towers. Others are small, like candleholders. They may be black, red, or gray. Everything's made of a hard stone called granite.

You're visiting Willis Granite Products in Granite. It's near the Wichita Mountains. These mountains are mostly made of granite.

Granite, limestone, and coal are mined in Oklahoma. But oil and natural gas are even more important. They're Oklahoma's top mining products.

Many Oklahoma factories help the oil industry. They make machines used to drill for oil. Other factories make airplanes, cars, or computers.

Many natural resources are mined in Oklahoma.

When August comes, head for Anadarko. You'll get to see the American Indian Expo. Thousands of Native Americans gather there every year.

This festival lasts for six days. It celebrates the arts, crafts, and customs of 13 Plains Native American tribes. You'll see some amazing dances. The dancers wear colorful feathers, beads, and fringe.

The event also has a carnival, games, parades, and talent contests. Visitors can learn the history of the present-day Native American tribes in Oklahoma. Thousands of people attend the American Indian Expo every year.

Oklahoma's Kiowa Tribe celebrates its ancestors with a powwow.

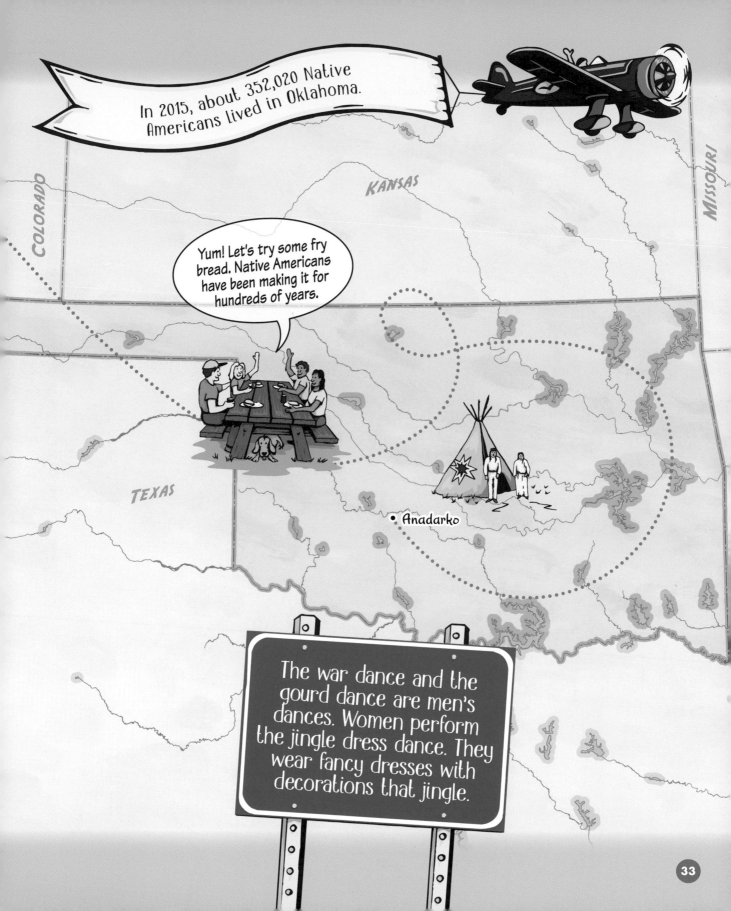

In 2015, about 352,020 Native Americans lived in Oklahoma.

Yum! Let's try some fry bread. Native Americans have been making it for hundreds of years.

COLORADO

KANSAS

MISSOURI

TEXAS

• Anadarko

The war dance and the gourd dance are men's dances. Women perform the jingle dress dance. They wear fancy dresses with decorations that jingle.

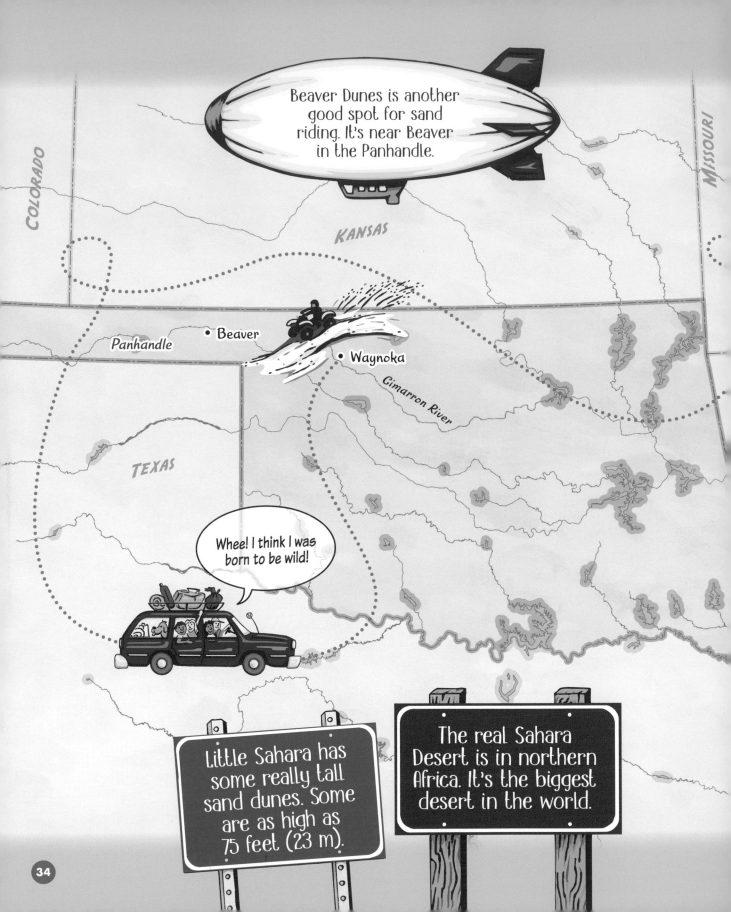

Beaver Dunes is another good spot for sand riding. It's near Beaver in the Panhandle.

COLORADO

MISSOURI

KANSAS

Panhandle

• Beaver

• Waynoka

Cimarron River

TEXAS

Whee! I think I was born to be wild!

Little Sahara has some really tall sand dunes. Some are as high as 75 feet (23 m).

The real Sahara Desert is in northern Africa. It's the biggest desert in the world.

Hop in your **dune** buggy. Strap on your helmet and buckle up. Soon you're flying across a sea of sand!

Zoom up a sand dune and zigzag down. Take twisty trails through sandy woods. See people lining up at the drag strip? They're getting ready to race!

You're at Little Sahara near Waynoka. It's a desert with tall sand dunes. Some people call it a great big sandbox!

The Cimarron River used to cover this area. Over thousands of years, the river shrank. It left tons of sand behind. All the more fun for you!

A dune buggy races through the sand at Little Sahara.

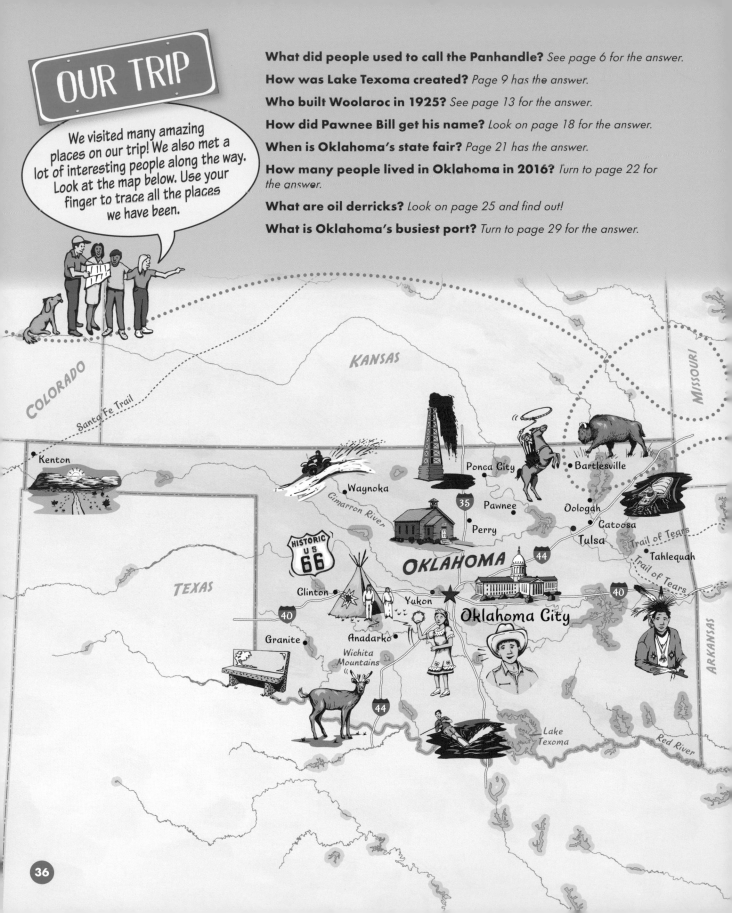

OUR TRIP

We visited many amazing places on our trip! We also met a lot of interesting people along the way. Look at the map below. Use your finger to trace all the places we have been.

What did people used to call the Panhandle? *See page 6 for the answer.*

How was Lake Texoma created? *Page 9 has the answer.*

Who built Woolaroc in 1925? *See page 13 for the answer.*

How did Pawnee Bill get his name? *Look on page 18 for the answer.*

When is Oklahoma's state fair? *Page 21 has the answer.*

How many people lived in Oklahoma in 2016? *Turn to page 22 for the answer.*

What are oil derricks? *Look on page 25 and find out!*

What is Oklahoma's busiest port? *Turn to page 29 for the answer.*

COLORADO

KANSAS

MISSOURI

Santa Fe Trail

Kenton

Waynoka

Cimarron River

HISTORIC US 66

TEXAS

Clinton

40

Granite

Anadarko

Wichita Mountains

Yukon

35

Ponca City

Bartlesville

Pawnee

Perry

Oologah

Catoosa

Tulsa

Trail of Tears

Tahlequah

Trail of Tears

OKLAHOMA

44

Oklahoma City

40

ARKANSAS

44

Lake Texoma

Red River

STATE SYMBOLS

State animal: American buffalo (bison)

State beverage: Milk

State bird: Scissor-tailed flycatcher

State butterfly: Black swallowtail

State country-and-western song: "Faded Love"

State fish: White bass (sand bass)

State floral emblem: Mistletoe

State folk dance: Square dance

State game animal: White-tailed deer

State game bird: Wild turkey

State grass: Indian-grass

State insect: Honeybee

State musical instrument: Fiddle

State poem: "Howdy Folks" by David Randolph Milsten

State rock: Rose rock

State theater: Lynn Riggs Players of Oklahoma

State tree: Redbud

State waltz: "Oklahoma Wind"

State wildflower: Indian blanket

STATE SONG

"OKLAHOMA!"

From the musical Oklahoma!

Words by Oscar Hammerstein II, music by Richard Rodgers

Brand new state! Brand new state, gonna treat you great!
Gonna give you barley, carrots and pertaters,
Pasture fer the cattle, spinach and termayters!
Flowers on the prairie where the June bugs zoom,
Plen'y of air and plen'y of room,
Plen'y of room to swing a rope!
Plen'y of heart and plen'y of hope.

Oklahoma, where the wind comes sweepin' down the plain,
And the wavin' wheat can sure smell sweet
When the wind comes right behind the rain.
Oklahoma, ev'ry night my honey lamb and I
Sit alone and talk and watch a hawk makin' lazy circles in the sky.
We know we belong to the land
And the land we belong to is grand!
And when we say—Yeeow! A-yip-i-o-ee ay!
We're only sayin'
You're doin' fine, Oklahoma!
Oklahoma—O.K.!

That was a great trip! We have traveled all over Oklahoma! There are a few places that we didn't have time for, though. Next time, we plan to visit Swan Lake Park in Tulsa. Visitors can view several different types of swans, geese, and ducks. Some of the birds are difficult to spot in the wild. But you can easily study them at the park!

State flag

State seal

FAMOUS PEOPLE

Aikman, Troy (1966–), football player

Bench, Johnny (1947–), baseball player

Brooks, Garth (1962–), country music singer

Ernst, Lisa Campbell (1957–), children's author and illustrator

Guthrie, Woody (1912–1967), country and folk music singer

Hanson, Ike (1980–), **Taylor** (1983–), **Zak** (1985–), pop music singers

Hillerman, Tony (1925–2008), author

Houser, Allan (1914–1994), Apache sculptor

Howard, Ron (1954–), actor and director

Lucid, Shannon (1943–), retired astronaut

Mankiller, Wilma (1945–2010), Cherokee chief

Mantle, Mickey (1931–1995), baseball player

McEntire, Reba (1955–), country music singer

Miller, Shannon (1977–), Olympic gymnast

Pitt, Brad (1963–), actor

Sequoyah (ca. 1776–1843), Cherokee leader

Shelton, Blake (1976–), country music singer, songwriter, television personality

Smith, Lane (1959–), children's author and illustrator

Tallchief, Maria (1925–2013), dancer and choreographer

Thorpe, Jim (ca. 1888–1953), Olympic athlete

Underwood, Carrie (1983–), country music singer, songwriter

Warren, Elizabeth (1949–), politician

WORDS TO KNOW

barges (BARJ-ez) long, flat boats that carry heavy goods

blowguns (BLOH-guhnz) hunting weapons made of a narrow tube through which a dart is blown

boom towns (BOOM TOUNZ) towns that grew quickly because of a new business activity

chaps (CHAPS) wide leather strips that protect the legs of cowboys when they ride

culture (KUHL-chur) a people's customs, beliefs, and way of life

descendants (di-SEND-uhnts) children, grandchildren, greatgrandchildren, and so on

dune (DOON) a high mound of sand

immigrants (IM-uh-gruhnts) people who leave their home country and move to another country

industry (IN-duh-stree) a type of business

mesa (MAY-suh) a high, flat-topped hill

plains (PLAYNZ) stretches of fairly flat land

preserve (pri-ZURV) a place that protects wild animals

territory (TER-uh-tor-ee) an area of land, often having definite borders

TO LEARN MORE

IN THE LIBRARY

Aronin, Miriam. *Oklahoma's Devastating May 2013 Tornado*. New York, NY: Bearport Publishing, 2014.

Garland, Sherry. *Voices of the Dust Bowl*. Gretna, LA: Pelican Publishing Company, 2012.

Saylor-Marchant, Linda. *Oklahoma*. New York, NY: Children's Press, 2009.

Simermeyer, Genevieve. *Meet Christopher: An Osage Indian Boy from Oklahoma*. Tulsa, OK: Council Oak Books, 2008.

ON THE WEB
Visit our Web site for links about Oklahoma:
childsworld.com/links

Note to Parents, Teachers, and Librarians: We routinely verify our Web links to make sure they are safe and active sites. So encourage your readers to check them out!

PLACES TO VISIT OR CONTACT
Oklahoma Historical Society
okhistory.org
800 Nazih Zuhdi Drive
Oklahoma City, OK 73105
405/521-2491
For more information about the history of Oklahoma

Travel Oklahoma
travelok.com
900 North Stiles Avenue
Oklahoma City, OK 73104-3234
800/652-6552
For more information about traveling in Oklahoma

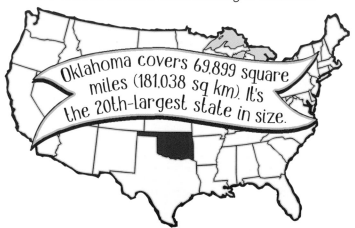

Oklahoma covers 69,899 square miles (181,038 sq km). It's the 20th-largest state in size.

INDEX

Bye, Sooner State. We had a great time. We'll come back soon!